Officer Brown Keeps Neighborhoods Safe

written by
ALICE K. FLANAGAN

photographs by
CHRISTINE OSINSKI

Reading Consultant
LINDA CORNWELL
Learning Resource Consultant
Indiana Department of Education

CHILDREN'S PRESS®   *A Division of Grolier Publishing*
New York • London • Hong Kong • Sydney • Danbury, Connecticut

Special thanks to Officer Deborah Hawes-Brown
for allowing us to tell her story.

Officer Brown wishes to dedicate this book to
Elliott (Kip) A. Jenkins, Jr.

Library of Congress Cataloging-in-Publication Data
Flanagan, Alice.
   Officer Brown keeps neighborhoods safe / written by Alice K.
Flanagan / photographs by Christine Osinski ; reading consultant,
Linda Cornwell.
      p. cm. — (Our neighborhood series)
   Summary: Introduces a female deputy chief of the Hartford,
Connecticut, Police and discusses the things she is expected to do in her
job.
   ISBN 0-516-20780-6 (lib. bdg.)   0-516-26407-9 (pbk.)
   1. Police—Juvenile literature. 2. Occupations. [1. Police. 2.
Occupations.] I. Osinski, Christine, ill. II. Title. III. Series: Our neigh-
borhood series (New York, N.Y.)
HV7922.F58 1998
363.2'023'73—dc21   97-49378
                                                       CIP
                                                       AC

Photographs ©: Christine Osinski

Officer Deborah Hawes-Brown is a deputy chief of the Hartford, Connecticut, Police Department. She helps the chief of police.

Officer Brown was not always a deputy chief. First, she was a patrol officer.

She drove a police car through
neighborhoods. She and her partner
kept people safe.

Sometimes, they stopped fights and arrested people for breaking the law.

If Officer Brown needed help, she called the police station on her radio. The station sent more officers.

HARTFORD POLICE
ACADEMY

AMPHITHEATER →

Officer Brown trained to be a police officer at the Hartford Police Academy. There, she learned about the law.

She learned to think quickly and act carefully.

She learned how to solve problems
and help people in trouble.

She learned to use a radio,

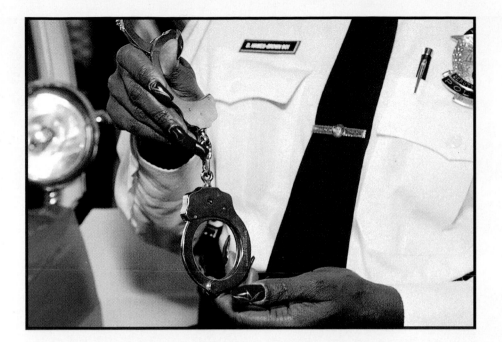

handcuffs,

and a club.

She learned to wear a bulletproof
vest . . .

. . . and how to shoot a gun.

Cloe Poisson / The Hartford Courant

■ Elliott Jenkins of Bloomfield pins a Hartford deputy police chief's badge on the shirt of his daughter, Deborah Hawes-Brown, at her swearing-in ceremony Thursday at the city's police headquarters. She is the highest-ranking female police officer in the state.

For Hartford officer, a badge of high honor

By LIZABETH HALL
Courant Correspondent

The attention that comes from breaking gender barriers shouldn't have bothered Deborah Hawes-Brown, but the moments before her appointment as a Hartford deputy police chief left her pacing the floor.

The meditative quiet she had hoped for was impossible amid the crush of hugs, handshakes and pointed greetings of "Hi, chief." Cornered as she was, Hawes-Brown politely submitted as a male subordinate straightened her gold tie pin in preparation for the horde of people and news cameras she would soon face for her swearing-in ceremony.

All were on hand to acknowledge Hawes-Brown as the first woman in any Connecticut police department to attain a rank with the word "chief" in her title.

Next to Hawes-Brown, the highest-ranking female police officer in Connecticut is a captain in the state police.

In her rise through Hartford's police department, the largest municipal force in Connecticut, Hawes-Brown's record is filled with firsts: first black female sergeant, first female lieutenant, first female captain.

Her appearance in the training classroom, where swearing-in ceremonies are traditionally held, brought the kind of greeting found at the start of an Oprah Winfrey show.

Amid the standing ovation, exultant friends shouted "You go, girl!" and raised fists toward the ceiling. The ceremony drew police officers; members of her church, Faith Congregational; her family; and people from the community who appreciated help she has given them.

Barely audible above the cheers, Chief Joseph F. Croughwell Jr. said the cross section that turned out for her promotion exemplified his reasons for promoting her to his inner circle. She will replace Deputy Chief Tom O'Connor, who is retiring after 23 years to become director of security at Travelers Group

Inc.

"We are involved in community-oriented policing and she is dedicated to that," Croughwell said. "It isn't unusual for someone to come up to me and tell me what a great job she's doing. Her expertise, her knowledge and her goodness really go beyond this police department."

Hawes-Brown, 41, joined the department in 1974 as a cadet. She became a fully sworn officer after attending what was then the all-male police academy in Meriden in 1976. She rose to sergeant in 1982, lieutenant in 1990 and captain last year.

The honor of pinning her gold-adorned deputy's badge to her crisp white shirt fell to Hawes-Brown's father, Elliott Jenkins.

Hawes-Brown had kept her interest in police work a secret, knowing that he would disapprove, Jenkins said. He was tipped off by a neighbor who was interested in knowing why

Please see Female, Page A15

Today, Officer Brown is the highest-ranking female officer in Connecticut. She works in an office. She doesn't patrol the streets anymore.

As a deputy chief, Officer Brown is in charge of safety in the central part of the city. She sends out police officers to control traffic and stop street crime.

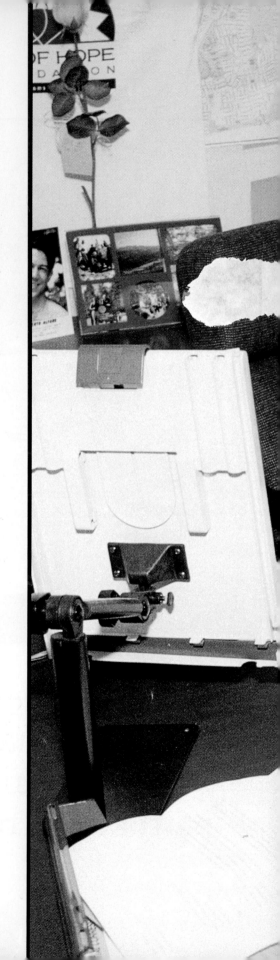

Two special people help Officer Brown in her job.

Officer Paulina gives the police officers their work orders.

Officer Adams makes sure the officers on the street do their jobs well.

Some police officers patrol neighborhoods on bikes.

Other officers ride horses . . .

. . . or patrol with dogs.

Sometimes, Officer Brown works with people in neighborhoods to stop crime before it happens.

Officer Brown visits schools and talks to children.

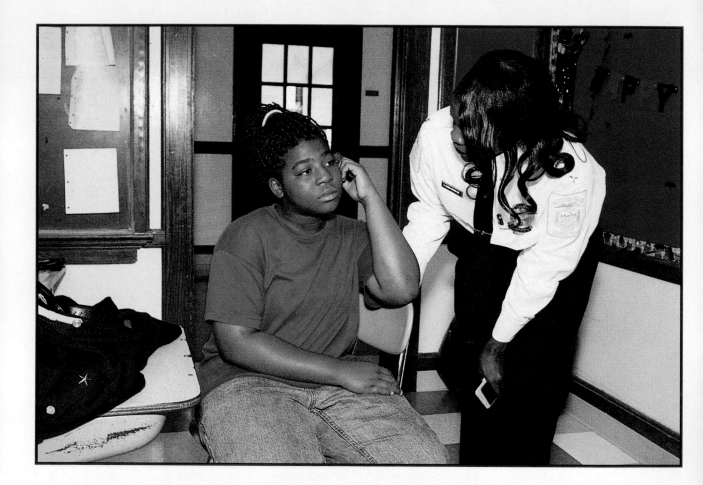

She tells them: "Respect yourselves and stay in school."

"Don't look for heroes in gangs.
Say no to drugs and follow your
dreams."

Officer Brown's parents taught her
to respect people and to help those
in need. Now, as a police officer, she
does both.

She and her husband pass on these values to their children, too.

Officer Deborah Hawes-Brown is a good police officer. She cares about people. She is honest and fair.

She does her
best to keep
neighborhoods
safe.

Meet the Author
and the Photographer

Alice Flanagan and Christine Osinski are sisters. They grew up together telling stories and drawing pictures in a brown brick bungalow in a southwest-side neighborhood of Chicago, Illinois. Today they write stories and take photographs professionally.

Ms. Flanagan resides in Chicago with her husband and works as a freelance writer. Ms. Osinski is a photographer and teaches at The Cooper Union for the Advancement of Science and Art in New York City. She lives with her husband and two sons in Ridgefield, Connecticut.